Life

BEFORE *and* AFTER

DNA

Tina Louise Jones

ISBN 979-8-89130-872-5 (paperback)
ISBN 979-8-89130-873-2 (digital)

Christian Faith Publishing
832 Park Avenue
Meadville, PA 16335
www.christianfaithpublishing.com

Printed in the United States of America

You know every step my journey will
take before my journey begins.

—Psalm 139; paraphrased

Before I formed thee in the belly I knew thee; and before thou camest forth out of the womb I sanctified thee, and I ordained thee a prophet unto the nations.

—Jeremiah 1:5 KJV

I WENT THROUGH THE MOST painful rejection of my life. Now I focus on what matters, and that's who stood with me, often holding me up during those times when most all departed. I'm grateful for my husband, sons and their families, friends too numerous to mention, and my ex-husband (most people can't thank their *exes* for standing with them through adverse times; however, when most of my family left, he came to defend me, for which my husband and I are both grateful), and most importantly God, who has been with me all the way. He knew I knew He would never leave nor forsake me, as He promised in scripture. Even though it was a most heartbreaking time for me, I never felt alone.

Chapter 1

WHERE DO I START, except at the beginning. For me, the beginning starts with my first memories. Those memories, like anyone else, is the beginning of our personality formation, or is it?

I'm just a girl still living in my hometown. I have a family whom I love and adore with all my heart. Some members of my family, I've recently discovered, through the most difficult of times, are void of those same loving and caring feelings toward me; however, that wasn't always the case, or so it seemed. So what happened?

All because of DNA…

I stumbled on the most logical probability because of the whispers in the dark by those who proclaim to know a secret, a secret I've only recently heard about, and it's the darkest, most painful reality for the one targeted—and that's me.

I'm sharing my journey with those who choose to read my story, since all those who were close to me all my life are now distant through no fault of my own.

I'm so thankful for my amazing, loving, and sympathetic husband. Without him and his support, I doubt I'd still be standing.

I was an extremely quiet and nervous child. Some have shared, it was very evident early on I was while others actually believed I felt I was too good to talk with them, which is so far from the truth. I pray that if that was the case, they'll read the words of my story and realize that was not the case. The only thing I avoided was dramatic issues. Somehow, I learned early in life, drama was not a friend.

My first recollection is when I was probably around four or five years old and my daddy was riding me on his back while he was on all fours. I remember he did this often, and when he didn't have a shirt on, I always said I got my freckles off my daddy's back. I also remember, around the age seven or eight, playing school upstairs in the old farmhouse we lived in at the time, just me and my dolls.

I also remember loving school; reading was my favorite. When my mother took me to the library, which she often did, I would always gravitate to the books on nursing. Nurses held a fascination with me because of their attention to detail in helping the doctors in such a caring way to help their patients recover. This view of nursing was a driving force for my goals when I got older. I knew I wanted to be a nurse, but then a life-altering event happened—a bicycle wreck! Some may think that wouldn't be a life-altering event, but to me it was. When my mother had spent hours picking all the pea gravel embedded into my bloody knees, this event changed the direction of my future desires. The sight of blood, much like drama, I found, was not my friend. I even experienced passing out when blood was drawn for my monthly checkup during my first pregnancy. The ammonia they used as an inhalant under my nose worked wonders, by the way, wink (smile), but it also was not my friend. Shew, that stuff stinks!

We used to have a family night on Saturdays. I remember Mom would bake a cake and make home-made icing to put on it. I recall a couple of my uncles (my daddy's brothers) coming over, and the grown-ups would play rummy while us kids would lay in the floor in front of the TV and watch *Hee Haw*, *Hollywood Squares*, *The Lawrence Welk Show*, and whatever came on after that.

I also remember, in the summertime while school was out, Mom would take me, my sister, and my brother to Mamaw's house (Dad's mom) and drop us off because she had something to do. She sold Avon at that time, as other women did. My aunts (my daddy's sisters) would take us walking down the road to the creek, and we would take off our shoes and go wading in the creek. I was always looking out for snakes, but this one time, there was a *huge* crawfish getting ready to bite my big toe, and that was the last time I got in the creek. I'm not one that likes going barefoot anyway.

I remember going over to Mamaw's house (Dad's mom) on Sunday nights to eat supper. She could really cook! My cousin and I would go outside and play with our dolls under the big tree next to the road on the big rock. Back then, even though we didn't feel unsafe regarding traffic on our road, we just knew that the asphalt road wasn't a playground.

I recall a sunny day outside, playing with my brother and sister then suddenly witnessing my sister climbing a tree and getting her foot hung in between two limbs. She eventually got free; however, it was a very scary few minutes for us all. On another occasion, a Sunday afternoon, while our dad was playing with us—as he often did uneventfully—this day, however, he became like an older mischievous brother. Often he would have us take a blade of grass and touch the electric fence to make sure it was on. But this day he handed me a fly swat that had a metal handle and told me to touch the fence. I touched the fence, and as quickly as I did, I ended up on the ground, looking at the sky on my back! What we didn't think about was, I had on sandals with metal rings on the top of both feet. That encounter with the fly swat, fence, and sandals has not been forgotten after all these years, nor was the laughter from him and me after we realized I had survived. Needless to say, I avoided electric fences from then on. Adventures were always on the menu in our family, like the big black snake we noticed in our big old oak tree in our backyard, but it wasn't there long, as Dad quickly went into the house and exited with a gun. One shot, and it slowly fell to the ground.

Chapter 2

MY DAD MAY NOT have had a typical education like most, only to the eighth grade, yet he was the smartest man I knew. When he quit school and until he got married, he worked to help his family. After working many years for others, he decided to start his own carpentry business. He had enough experience from years prior, building homes, remodeling, as well as other similar jobs. He did so well he had two crews all working different jobs at the same time. Though he owned the business, he acted as gopher to each of his crews. Whatever they needed, he would go for it. He was a great leader and boss and, as I mentioned earlier, a very smart man.

Dad built our home, the one I grew up in. We all helped by carrying bricks, using the grout trowel to make the groove between the bricks, or whatever help he needed us to do. Nothing was off-limits, not even the roof. Dad was putting shingles on, and all us kids were up there with him when I stumbled and nearly fell off the back of the house. Needless to say, I never climbed the roof again, nor to this day will I do heights. As I recall my dad and his abilities, I also remember the numerous homes he built for families from the ground up, as well as remodels; but I also remember him doing work for the many substations for the local utilities, remodeling for particular banks and some of the county and city churches in the area.

My dad could build anything he set his mind to.

One year I received a typewriter; can't remember if it was for my birthday or Christmas, but either way, I would type letters to my aunt that lived in Rogersville. I learned how to address an envelope, and it was exciting waiting for the mailman to run to see if I had received a letter back from her.

I also remember, during this time, I had the privilege to be a participant in the county fair pageant, Fairest of the Fair. I had my hair curled, was dressed up, and wore long white gloves and a two-toned-brown dress. I was so excited but nervous! In fact, I was about as nervous as I was when I nearly fell off the roof! Of course, I didn't place, but it was a fun and exciting experience.

One particular Christmas, I remember all I wanted was a ski jacket. I'm guessing I wanted one because everyone at school had one. It was all I wanted. On Christmas morning, as usual, we all jumped up and ran to open our gifts, and no ski jacket. I was so disappointed to the point of being upset; nothing

I received that day mattered. It helped knowing my aunt and uncle were coming with their children to eat lunch. I had forgotten we all had drawn names. My aunt handed me my present. I opened it—it was my ski jacket. I was more than happy. I was ecstatic. I wore it every chance I could.

Chapter 3

IN THE SUMMER, WE and most everyone we knew always put out tobacco. We definitely weren't rich, so Daddy did it to help with the family finances, as he didn't like being indebted to anyone. One thing I realize now is, we never went without. We learned how to work hard for what we wanted.

Most everyone dreaded working in tobacco because, they said, it was so much work. It certainly was, but for some reason, I loved it—that is, for the most part. I enjoyed pulling the plants. I loved riding the setter, especially with my uncle Terry. I often thought we were a team, and a very good team at that. The part I didn't like was chopping the tobacco out. If I could have, I would have skipped out on that part, along with topping and suckering. Then the next step came, cutting it. I was all in as long as I had a partner that could "spud" fast. My personal drive was actually a private game I played. That game was to get to the far side of the rows faster than anyone else and not leaving many leaves to be picked up in my rows. My memory also recalls one winter, while doing tobacco, my daddy was helping me learn my multiplication facts while pulling the tobacco off in the barn; it made learning fun. My dad was so smart. He knew figures and always made learning easier.

When Uncle Terry passed away, I saw my dad hurting. They weren't just brothers. They were partners and had been working together for years. He took off work that day, and so did I. Days later, we worked together in the garden, just him and me. There wasn't much talking, just working.

As I grow older, I see so many similarities. I often feel I'm just like my dad in many ways. When he hurt, he just wanted to be alone. I find I'm that way too. I guess it's a way we can figure how to deal with our pain our own way. I've also found, when we're alone, it makes a clearer path to hear from God. He can get us through in a way no one else can.

With all the wisdom my sweet dad had, his one liability was, he couldn't read. I remember the day he asked me to teach him. The Bible was my choice to teach him from. Slowly he learned words and would even pick up and read the newspaper at times, not fully but enough to understand.

Dad and I always voted together. He never voted for someone without detailing things about them. Dad always wanted to vote for the right reasons. We always went to vote together, and the officials always let me go with Dad to help him with the process of voting. These are some wonderful memories. I enjoyed those times with him.

Chapter 4

Every year, we always had a pretty huge garden and canned as much as possible and put some items in the freezer. In the summer, Mom's sister, the one I wrote letters to, would come and stay with us. She didn't drive and would help Mom can and freeze the food. It seemed like when we were in the garden, Mom or her sisters would make a remark about me being found under a cabbage leaf. Not sure why, but I just went along with it. A few times my aunts (Mom's sisters) would ask me why I don't look like my sister or brother. Well, I didn't know what to say except probably because I was found under a cabbage leaf. I remember in health class learning about how the different genes would determine the eye color of a person. They would just laugh like it was some kind of joke or something. At the time, I had no idea what was going on. Funny thing is, years later, I would find those jokes weren't jokes at all. They were actually leading up to a painful but major hidden truth since before my birth and about my life. I guess they were trying to tell me something without actually telling me. Who knows… If anyone—I don't care who you are—if you have kept a secret for fifty-one years, take it to the grave with you, period. It makes no sense telling and ruining several families' lives.

Chapter 5

I WAS ALWAYS RAISED IN church and have always believed that Jesus is the Son of God. He died for our sins and rose the third day. I asked God into my life at an early age but also confessed in front of witnesses and got baptized along with my soon-to-be husband at the time. We got married, bought a house, and the first thing I carried in was my Bible. I wanted to make sure God was first and foremost in our lives. I was working two jobs at the time, and in a couple of years, we had our son, Cody. Everything was wonderful until it seemed my husband didn't want to be married any longer.

One day in 1991, sitting at a red light—I will never forget—it hit me, and hit me hard enough to open my eyes.

Shortly, I attended a revival, I again went to the altar and rededicated my life to Christ. It appears I have a desire every time something drastic happens in my life, feeling the overwhelming need to "re-rededicate" my life and start over.

While we both loved our son, I wasn't blind to the fact something had changed between us. Soon we followed the path of many and divorced. When we went to court, that day ended our marriage in the year 1992. Shortly after my divorce, I met Mike. We dated a couple of years, and we married in December 1994. We have a son together named Kevin, born in 1996.

You were built for the battles assigned to you.

Chapter 6

1999 WAS THE YEAR we started building our house and moved in, in the fall of 2000. We did most of it ourselves through the week and then on Saturdays, and for that reason, it took much longer to finish. We even cut the trees and had them cut up, plain down and tongue and grooved. We did all the sanding and staining ourselves. It was a lot of work, but well worth it. During this time of building the house was when we found out that Mike was sick. He was bad sick. Didn't know for sure what was going on but knew something was happening with him.

We visited a number of neurologists. The first one surmised Mike had ALS, so for a year, we lived believing that. We were then sent to a doctor who was originally from India but now lived and practiced in Johnson City, Tennessee, about thirty to forty minutes away from where we lived. He stated after many tests, he had never witnessed anything like what Mike had in the fifteen years of his practice and had no real understanding of what Mike had. He then sent us to a physician in Knoxville. After hearing and reading what Mike was going through, Doctor Thomas was determined to find out what was wrong with Mike. The first thing Doctor Thomas did was remove three inches of nerve from the outside of Mike's left ankle and conducted a test on it. Upon his return to the room, we were anxiously awaiting him and his findings. As he stepped into the room, he stated with complete understanding of Mike's condition. The condition is called Charco-Marie-Tooth disease. I, like Sarah in the Bible, chuckled simply because I had thought he was joking or, like the other doctor, was completely clueless and offering anything as a possibility even through a joke. I quickly found out he wasn't joking, and it wasn't what it sounded like, as in a tooth disease. Doctor Thomas went on to share, Mike's condition was in the family of MS (multiple sclerosis) and MD (muscular dystrophy) family. Doctor Thomas also shared it was hereditary. He asked if we would like to get Kevin, our five-year-old son at the time, tested, but we declined. He mentioned to watch for weakness and to consider getting him tested when he was older, but added, it often skips generations. We aren't aware of any of Mike's family having the condition unless it went undiagnosed. Since being diagnosed, Mike has had countless surgeries just so he could continue to do simple, everyday things. One typical surgery for his condition was to remove a nerve from one finger to be rerouted to another—such as his forefinger and thumb—for the purpose of gaining more strength. Just think how easy it is to slide a debit card in at the pumps to get gas and pull it back out. Not so easy for someone with this disease. Also, holding a fork to eat—another not-so-easy task.

Unfortunately, however, on another occasion, a doctor had to surgically remove a finger that had become very infected. Another time, a toe had to be removed. Mike has had multiple surgeries on his feet to help with walking. His left ankle had gotten so bad and weak it had leaned over so much it actually touched the floor as he walked. We were guided to Mission's Hospital in Asheville, North Carolina. After several corrective surgical procedures, they finally used a Valor nail as a last resort before amputation through his heel into his leg to steady and hold it up straighter.

Lots of other surgeries followed, such as having tendons cut under his toes to help make them relax while loosening the hammertoes he was experiencing and relieve the issue of sores that caused frequent and painful infections. Once COVID-19 shots were suggested and given, he began to have what seemed to be issues with his heart and at one point even thought he was experiencing a heart attack and visited the ER. His heart checked out fine, which we were extremely relieved about. Shortly thereafter he had to have cataract surgery and then, if that wasn't enough, found he had a nodule on his thyroid, which led to the removal of half of his thyroid gland. During the surgery, it was found that the nodule was so large it had moved his trachea over to one side and was causing his breathing issues. I was with fear of losing my husband during this ordeal, but God saw us through it.

Just recently, Mike had to have another surgery on his leg. The Valor nail broke and also caused a bone in his leg to break. We feared the worse, thinking it would be amputation, but once the doctor did the X-ray, he said that he believed he could fix it without amputation. That was the best news. They set a time for the surgery. It took around five hours. It took an hour and a half to get the Valor nail out of his leg, then they put in a big plate and screws. He is currently healing from this surgery.

When God puts you together for better or for worse, in sickness and in health, you better take those vows to heart. He isn't kidding.

Chapter 7

Around 2001, I was taking my oldest son to youth group and dropping him off at church, and my younger son would start crying because he wanted to go to church with his brother. I explained to him that he couldn't because he was too young. Sunday after Sunday he would cry, wanting to go with his brother. The Lord laid it upon my heart at that time that maybe the church should have a younger group for the other kids that couldn't go. I prayed about it because if you know me, I'm like, "No, Lord, not me." Let me tell you something, when the Lord lays something on your heart, you might as well give in and just do it. So I asked one of my friends if she would help me, and she said yes. Next, I contacted the youth leaders and asked if it would be okay to have a youth group for the smaller kids. I mentioned how Kevin would cry every time I dropped Cody off, and she said that sounded like a wonderful idea. So my friend, Michelle, and I started a smaller youth group and gave them a name of The Team Kids. We were going to work as a team and learn about Jesus. This became a hit as we had several kids in our group. If you have ever taught and have such a wide age range, you understand that as we grew in numbers, we had to make the decision after a couple of years to divide and see if someone else would take over The Team Kids, and we would now be called The Mission Kids. We were now on a mission to learn how to spread the gospel. Michelle and I even got both our husbands involved in helping us. We wanted to take mission trips, and we in fact took the kids on a mission trip to China around March 2005. It was a *wow* moment for all of us involved!

We fixed up the downstairs basement of the church to look like the inside of an airplane. We made their passports and asked a real missionary to come and speak to us. Even though our mission trip was to China, she had been a missionary in Africa for several years. She even taught us a couple of songs in Swahili. Michelle's husband had been to China for work, so he brought some items he had collected on his trips, and the missionary had brought some of her collections. The children and all the adults experienced an amazing, memory-filled trip to China without leaving the church. Although we had other mission trips, the one to China would be the most amazing mission trip beyond the borders of America. We were blessed to experience it.

Some of the other mission trips, though mostly random and local, were in-depth learning experiences. Like, for example, we would go and sit in the parking lot of a grocery store and have our lesson there or to a park or on a hike. One time we went to the graveyard. We would just go to random places and have our lesson, but they were all mission-related.

Several years later, we were moving up to the regular youth group and had someone take over the Mission Kids. We named the other two so we couldn't just be called the youth group. We decided on The Radical Generation (TRG). We continued this until our boys graduated high school and turned the reigns over to others, as we had been doing it for close to thirteen to fourteen years.

After being out of it for a while, a couple of the ladies asked me to help them, and so I did for another couple years until the accident, and I had to step back. I couldn't concentrate or stay focused like I should have.

Has God spoken to you?

Chapter 8

In 2010 I WAS getting up one morning and did a full body stretch in the bed. Something popped in my right knee. It didn't hurt, so I started to get up to get ready for work, and then I realized I couldn't straighten my right leg. As long as I kept it bent, it didn't hurt, but as soon as I tried to straighten it, I would be in tears. Mike took me to the ER, and when they x-rayed it, turns out the cartilage had flipped in my knee. I was then scheduled for knee surgery. After surgery, several days later, I developed a DVT (blood clot). I had to go back to the doctor and get an ultrasound that confirmed it. My family doctor couldn't treat a DVT. The surgeon couldn't treat a DVT. So the ER doctor had to admit me into the hospital so the nurses could show Mike how to give me the shots that would treat the blood clot and then released me.

After healing from that, a coworker knew my desire to go on a mission trip. I have always wanted to go to Africa. Not sure why, but it has held a special place in my heart for some reason. Only God knows why. My friend mentioned to me at work one day that their church was going on a mission trip to Belize and taking several people and wanted to know if I wanted to go. Oh, my heart said yes, but my mind was not so sure at the moment. Yes, of course, I would like to go, but, all the what-ifs started running through my mind. What if something happened to my family while I was that far away? What if my sister passed away? She was really sick and wasn't doing well. What if, what if, what if… I began praying, *God, if this is your will, You will make a way for me to go*. God knew what I was facing in the years to come that I didn't see. He knew I was on the fence about going on this mission trip. So I started praying, praying, and praying. *If it is your will, please give me a sign that everything and everybody will be okay while I'm gone. Please give me a sign that I and my family will be safe*. All day every day at work, I was praying.

One day, I had just gone to the ladies' room and just got through earnestly praying for a sign, and it was like I heard the voice of God say, "Go where I send thee." Never had I felt like I had heard the voice of God before or since then. "Go where I send thee." I haven't heard that song in years, let alone been thinking about it. I could not get that song out of my mind after that. My heart was heavy with worry before, but after that, I was at ease and felt very peaceful about everything. He knew what I needed. I told my friend yes and asked what I needed to do to get ready. She said, I had to raise funds, purchase my plane ticket, get shots, get a passport, and luggage. I went before my church to see if they would help raise funds for me, as I wanted my whole church involved in this mission trip, not just me. Shortly after, another young lady in my church decided she, too, wanted to be a part of this mission trip to Belize. The church followed with a fundraiser for both of us. We both went together and shared our mission trip, along with another church group. This was such a great, humbling experience. I truly enjoyed it and will never forget the people I met and the friendships made there.

After we returned back home, I realized how worried my husband and my sons were for me being so far away in another country. I wasn't that worried when we arrived that Friday. I was so hyped up and excited.

My dream of going on a mission trip was coming true, and I wanted to soak it all in. I took notes of what we did every day that we were there and everything we saw. It was a little confusing when we arrived in Belize and going through customs when they started questioning the other girl that went with me, though it must have been standard procedure, as we both were cleared finally. Then Sunday after our church service in Belize, it was our free day, and they took us to the Mayan Ruins. We had to get on a ferry to cross the river, and on the other side was an Army soldier with his gun that I didn't think too much about until we reached the very top and there was another one sitting on top of the ruins with his machine gun, and I asked one of our leaders what he was here for.

She said, "Oh, to protect us."

I said, "Protect us from what?"

She said, "Because Guatemala is right over there, and they sneak over the border to rob the tourists."

I said, "Oh!" Then I was like, "I'm not in Kansas anymore."

Even though that is just a phrase, that is exactly how I felt at that very moment. I thought, *This is not a vacation.* We were there to do work in another country for the less-privileged people. Let me tell you, everyone there looked like they needed help. They did what they had to do to survive. I have the most respect for all of them, as it was the most humbling experience I've ever been a part of. I am grateful for getting to go on this trip.

This lady from Honduras—I don't recall her name—I was drawn to her. The feeling was mutual, and we connected. I recall her husband was working, she had several children, and I learned that not all children in Belize had the benefit of attending school, only the ones that received sponsors. Even with her lacking essential things, she wanted to give me a gift. I didn't need it, but felt it was her way of showing me appreciation and confirming our friendship. I certainly didn't want to seem disrespectful. I still have it and remember her fondly because of it. She couldn't respond in English, but I knew her appreciation was heartfelt for the food we left for her and her family.

Chapter 9

My sister was two years younger than me and had six kids. She and her husband made me and her husband's brother guardians for their kids in case something happened to them. She was a good mother. You just had to know my sister to love her. She was good-hearted but had her ways about things. Often when she would get mad, she'd hold a grudge. The only remedy for that was to find something to make her laugh; it worked most every time. However, sometimes I found myself the mediator or counselor, depending on the need. Most times it was a simple misunderstanding.

My lifelong motto was about love, and love of family especially. My life proved and continues to prove my heart for family. I adore and love my nieces and nephews. They spent a lot of time with me, especially from the time they got off the bus on Fridays until I took them home after youth group on Sunday nights. I didn't just love my family. I was grateful for each and every one.

Over the next few years, my sister developed a lot of health issues, starting with fibromyalgia, arthritis, and strangely contracted a children's condition where her body broke out in red spots from her waist down. Her life consisted of a lot of medications, and she eventually ended up in a wheelchair. Sadly, renal failure, followed with the need of a kidney transplant. Unfortunately, her organs began to shut down before that life-saving event happened.

I recall the last conversation we had before she took her final trip to the hospital. She and her husband came by my house to drop the three youngest girls off. She took my hand and asked me to promise to homeschool the youngest girls. At that point, I realized her time was getting close. I promised her I would. I prayed and prayed often. My prayers were the pleading kind, begging for her to live. Her children needed her. I needed her.

The length of time she was in the hospital, I can't recall. All I do recall is the message I got: if I wanted to see her, I needed to go to the hospital now. I was numb. I kept working. I guess it was shock. Finally, reality hit me, and I announced, "I'm leaving. I have to go to the hospital." I couldn't believe I was losing my sister. I got there and immediately went in to see her, not prepared for what I was about to see. It was evident she wasn't doing well at all. *But* I couldn't nor wouldn't give up on her. She's strong. She'll pull through as she always has. Later that night we went in to see her and realized I needed to let go and say goodbye.

Shortly, she passed. All of a sudden, I felt so alone. I never had been or remember being without my sister.

Though I felt sorry for my loss, as I looked at her husband and their children, my pain was transferred from me to them. I wanted to hold and comfort each one to make everything okay, but nothing could make it okay. I just hoped each one would carry through their future years the knowledge of how much she loved them.

I kept my promise and homeschooled them for close to six months. I worked a full-time job, came in, picked the three girls up, went home, made supper, worked on homework, then would take them back home. They were okay to start with, and the longer it went on, they started displaying negative feelings toward me. I realize now they were over the cloudy space we all had been in since their mother's passing, and now were dealing with the pain in a way, as I look back now, as understandable. Their pain came out in statements often saying I wasn't their mother, so they didn't have to listen to me. I was an easy target to empty their feelings on, but I also knew this wasn't good for any of us and our relationship. I told their dad their expressed feelings toward me and gave him the option to do what he, as their dad, thought was best. Shortly he enrolled them in public school. I knew I had tried, but my relationship with them as their aunt was most important. I often checked on them and was extremely relieved each time they were doing really well.

Chapter 10

MY BROTHER IS THREE years younger than I was and also had six kids. I always enjoyed when the whole family could get together and have a meal. More times than not, they had other plans.

<h1 style="text-align:center">Chapter 11</h1>

I REMEMBER MOM ALWAYS ON the go. While we were younger, she sold Avon, and then as we got older, she started babysitting some of the neighborhood kids and my cousins. I have witnessed these children grow into adults and have tried to stay in contact with most of them, but like everyone, they have their own families now. Though there were many reliable and very respected daycares in our area, my mom decided she wanted to take care of Cody as she did with Kevin while I worked. Before Kevin started school, my mother and Mike's mother took turns until he started school. I was, as were my boys, fortunate that their grandparents weren't in the workforce, giving them the opportunity to spend quality time with them almost daily.

Mom loved to shop. Even while she was babysitting, she would take the kids with her to go shopping. She could make those kids mind no matter where they were. Even after Mom stopped babysitting, she started going to town just about every day. She loved bargain-hunting. She would find stuff on sale all the time, and when she found something she liked at a good price, she would purchase it in every color. No joke!

Mom developed so many health issues over the years and also ended up in a wheelchair. Rheumatoid and osteoarthritis, fibromyalgia, as well as diabetes afflicted her health majorly, but it didn't stop her from shopping. Now she used her credit card while watching HGTV and QVC channels. She had packages delivered daily. My mother's health was at a very serious stage. My dad took total care of every need she had, as well as all her doctor's appointments and hair appointments. He would come home from work to check on her, eat lunch, then go back to work. Then a desperate call came from my dad one night. She needed to go to the ER. We immediately went to their house and followed them to the hospital in Johnson City. I was so overwhelmed and prayed, *God, Your will be done.* I remember neither the ride to or from the hospital. As we stood there, watching the staff run tests on her, I recall feeling something was very wrong and remember saying, "I don't think she's breathing!" They immediately stopped what they were doing and checked. She wasn't breathing, and just like that, she was gone.

In Dad's grief, he asked me to call the preacher to let him know she was gone. I then called Mom's sister to let her know and asked her to share Mom had died with other family members. At this time in my life, I thought there was a lot of love from family. I was about to realize that wasn't the case, at least not as much as I had believed. It was hard, but we got through the heartbreak of losing Mom, followed by her funeral and her burial. Days later, UPS was delivering orders Mom had made prior to her death, so many, in fact, I finally had to call them to let them know she had died.

The companies worked with me to help discontinue deliveries while some even reimbursed her account. Funny thing was, Dad had deleted her credit card account because of the continuous orders and deliveries, but she found a way to get another credit card and continued what she enjoyed.

Chapter 12

AFTER MOM'S FUNERAL, MIKE and I tried our best to keep Dad busy. We also tried to lift his spirits, but he had lost her and therefore felt lost himself. A marriage of fifty-two years isn't easily forgotten nor easy to move on from. He loved her so much. Strangely, however, Dad started getting calls from female family members—requesting to take up residency in his house. Shocked was not even close to how he or I felt. I held my breath as I asked him how he responded to their requests. His response was, "No!"

Thank you, Jesus!

Chapter 13

Remembering through the years at Christmastime, Mom always made different kinds of candy and cookies for Daddy to take and deliver to the businesses that he dealt with a lot.

It was Christmas 2016, and Mom had passed away in February, so Dad decided to take around little poinsettias to a few people as Christmas gifts. He stopped at this little market that he must have been stopping at for a while to get breakfast. So he decided to give the cook, Alice, a poinsettia, ordered his biscuit, paid, and went to his truck. The cashier came out to his truck and said he needed to go back in and ask Alice out. Apparently, she had been watching their interaction for a while. He threw his biscuit across the seat and went back in and asked Alice out. A romance started all because of a poinsettia.

Then Dad wanted me to meet this lady he had been seeing, so he told me and Mike to meet them at

Ma and Pa's for supper one night. I was anxious and nauseated at the same time. I really didn't know how to feel. Yes, it had been a while since Mom passed away, but how was I supposed to feel about someone taking her place? I wasn't sure what or how to feel at the time, but if she was making my Daddy this happy, I was all for it. That was all I ever wanted—for my daddy to be happy.

We met at the restaurant, ate, talked, and laughed. I took their picture without them knowing it. When we were walking out of the restaurant, I snapped another picture because I saw my daddy holding Ms. Alice's hand. It was like they were high school sweethearts. I was so excited for them both. Remember, this was the first time I had met her. She invited us to go back over to her house, which wasn't far from the restaurant, and we did. After talking with her more, I found out I had met her years before at a store she had owned. Funny how life works out.

Everyone you meet along the way is for a reason.

Chapter 14

 IT WAS TIME TO go on vacation. Dad usually went unless we were going to the beach. He just wasn't that fond of the beach. I was wanting to go to the New England states, and he said yes, he would go—the last trip he would take with us since Mom passed away and before he and Alice would get married.

I had our trip pretty much planned out, noting what stops we needed to make in each state for some educational places I wanted us to see. We didn't get to make every stop I had planned, but we got to see most of them.

Just a few of the stops we made that were very impressive: Bar Harbor and Acadia National Park in Main, Mount Washington in New Hampshire, and the Mark Twain House in Connecticut, just to name a few of the places we visited.

It was a great trip. Dad even had me to take his picture at Bar Harbor, Maine, with the cruise ship in the background and him holding his cap over his heart and send it to Alice because he was missing her. How precious is that!

Dad and Alice had been dating several months, and Dad proposed, and of course, she said *yes*!

Now we are planning a wedding, shopping for a dress, decorating the church, and marriage in December 2017. About a week after the wedding, they left to take a cruise for their honeymoon trip.

Daddy moved into Alice's house, but he met me most every day at his house. I would stop to check the mail and answering machine. I would talk with Daddy for a while before he would leave and go home to Alice's. One afternoon, after I got off from work, as usual, I stopped at Dad's. I was surprised two of mom's sisters (my aunts, of course) were visiting Dad.

I looked at all of them, and Daddy said, "Girl, they have something to tell you."

I was like, "O-k-a-y…"

They proceeded to tell me that Dad was not my dad.

I was like, "What?"

They said it could be any of the three men they mentioned. I was shocked and really didn't have anything to say to them because, to me, why keep this a secret for fifty-one years and then tell it? What good did it do now?

Mark 3:35 (KJV) says, "Anyone who does God's will is my brother and sister and mother." Jesus explained that the relationships in our spiritual family are ultimately more important and longer-lasting than those in our physical families. (This verse is so true.)

It appeared Dad and I were hurt most of all. Later I told Daddy that if he wanted me to do a DNA test to confirm, I would. Otherwise, we would always have this suspicion now. I still couldn't believe this, so Daddy said to order the DNA test and we would all do it—him, my brother, and since my sister had already passed, her oldest daughter, and myself. Once the test kits came, I had everyone to swab the inside of their cheeks and place in the containers. I sent them off and awaited the results. I received the email in June on a Monday while at work. I remember this because it was the first night of Bible school in 2018. I called everyone and said for them to be at my house when I got off, and we will open them together, then

I had to get ready for Bible School. I still believed all three of the tests would show that we had the same dad. Once I started opening the test results, I was silently praying, *Please, Lord, if it's Your will, please let all the test results show that Dad is, in fact, our dad.* My sister's and brother's tests proved to be Dad's by 99.9 percent. When I opened my test, it stated 0 percent being Dad's. Dad and I both started crying. We were both so hurt. Dad was understandably hurt because he said he had asked Mom several different times if she was having an affair, and she always said no. I followed my daddy outside. He and I were both upset and crying. He told me right then that no matter what, he didn't want to be buried in the same plot where Mom was buried.

I told him, "Okay. If you want to be buried out where Alice has plots, that is fine. I will do my best to make sure that happens."

He then left my house, very visibly hurt and crying. I wasn't sure where he was going, but I asked if he would be okay, and he said he would be. I went back inside the house, and my brother asked for a copy of that test result. Really! Looking back now, I realize how painful that was. I would have hoped to hear, "I love you. No matter what, you're still my sis!" It was as if there was a tearing right down the middle of our life. He was on one side of that tear now, leaving me on the other. Everyone left, but I felt more alone when they all were there.

There's a message in the way a person treats you. Listen.

I started getting ready for Bible school. I broke down, total breakdown, as I headed to the church. I had to pull myself together, and once at church, I saw Daddy was there. That comforted me, seeing him and that he was okay. He was talking with the preacher. He wanted to make sure how I was doing. I went in and didn't mention anything, just started working. I couldn't break down there in front of all the kids and other adults. I felt like I had been slapped in the face. I wondered how long it would be before everyone knew about the news. I wondered how many people already knew. I was very self-conscious from that moment on. I started thinking maybe people already knew and they had been trying to figure out who I looked like. I was very self-conscious now.

Little did I know—but found out later—that after Dad had left my house, he went to the church up to the graveyard and scratched the pictures of him and Mom off the tombstone, crushed, and trashed them both. Then he went home and got cleaned up and went back to the church. After Bible school was over that first night, I went to the graveyard and asked Mom, "Why? Why would you do something like this and keep it a secret? I just don't understand." Then the tears started flowing. I went home, and I didn't know what to say to my family, or how I should feel. Five years later, and I'm still as blown away by this as ever. I feel like I have been walking in a fog. Although the fog has started to lift because God is putting the pieces of my heart back together. He is putting me back together, and I can tell I am a very different person than I was before. I have come to believe that God would not allow this pain into my life without a reason. I thought going through a divorce was the worst thing that could happen because it is worse than death, but this, *this* hurt way more. Being betrayed my whole life, and why now had this information need to be made known?

When you come into a storm, don't dodge it. Limp through it because the limp is your story.

Never in my wildest dreams would I have ever conceived what was about to happen to me and what would follow. Just the fact my own family, whom I had spent my whole life with, would disown me completely because of something I had no control of. It was painful enough to know and realize the secret my mother carried with her all my life, and she took it to the grave with her. My personal pain was deep, and my heart was shattered, not just for me but for my dad. There was no one feeling sorry for me and what I was going through silently and alone. You know one of two things can happen when you go through the darkest rivers in a storm— either you'll drown or you'll look for something to save you, something you can hold on to until you're safe. For me, that was Jesus. During that time, my dad, my sons and their family, my husband, and Jesus were all that I had and all that I needed.

Chapter 15

OCTOBER 10, 2018, A day I will never forget, the most hurt I had ever felt: the day we found out my daddy died.

It was like any other day. I talked with my daddy just about every morning on my way to work. I knew he had a couple of doctor appointments that morning. As usual, I stopped at Dad's after work to check the mail and answering machine. He would most always be there or come in shortly after I got there. We would talk for about thirty minutes, and then I would go home, and he would go to Alice's house.

This day after work was a little different. I came in and checked the mailbox and answering machine. I waited for a few minutes. His car was there, but I didn't really notice which vehicle was missing. So I just went on home, thinking Daddy had gone to check on the cows, and he would call me later. It wasn't thirty minutes after I got home that my phone rang, and it was Alice.

She said, "Tina, where is your daddy?"

I told her I didn't know because he wasn't at the house when I got there. She said that one of her daughters had been calling him all day, and he has never returned any of her phone calls. I thought that was odd, so I told her I would try to call him. I tried to call, and it went to voicemail. I told him to call me back. He wasn't answering, so I thought I needed to go look for him. I also called my brother. He said he was fixing supper and didn't know where Dad was, and that was the end of that conversation. So I went looking for Daddy. I stopped at his house again, and he wasn't there. The car was… I went over to the barn, and he wasn't there. I drove past the apartments, and he wasn't there either. I went back to Dad's, called my brother again, who said he hasn't talked to him and didn't know where he was. I called my husband, and he said that Dad had mentioned the night before he was going to get a load of rock. So I went driving over toward the rock quarry to see if maybe he had run off the road or had stopped to talk with someone. Got to the rock quarry, turned around, and came back the same way, looking off both sides of the road. Nothing. Went back to the barn, down to the hayfield, out by the apartments again. I was getting frantic now. I was very worried something was wrong, yet I was trying to stay calm. Drove back to the quarry, saw a worker coming out, and I asked him if maybe he had seen my daddy. He asked what color truck was he driving. I told him white. I left and was going back, just turned off onto Doughty's Chapel Road, and this man started blowing his horn at me. I stopped in the middle of the road, got out, and he yelled there was a white dump truck back down the road across from the quarry. I said thanks and went back, but it was a tandem dump truck, not my daddy's. I went back again and turned onto the Doughty's Chapel Road, and then I passed my brother.

He stopped and said, "Find him yet?"

I said, "No."

He said, "Maybe he took the dump truck to Walmart to get new tires."

I said, "I don't know."

He said he would drive up that way and see. My oldest son called me as I was stopping at Daddy's house. He told me to call Verizon and have them ping his phone to get a location of where he was.

As I started to call Verizon, my brother called and wanted to know where I was, and I said, "Dad's house. Why?"

He wanted to know if I was alone, and I said, "Yes, why?"

He said, "I found him."

I asked, "Where?"

He said, "Up here on the side of the hill. The truck ran over him."

I said, "No! Is he okay?"

He said, "He is gone."

My whole life was shattered into pieces. I loved my daddy so much. We called the preacher, and they put it on the prayer chain at church. We called Alice, and she was on her way as were others to give their support after hearing what had happened.

The time that followed from that dreadful day, October 10, 2018, until present has been a blur.

We went to the funeral home to make preparations for Daddy's burial, and I made sure to keep my promise to Daddy that he was not to be buried where Mom was buried but where Alice had plots, with Alice's approval, of course. After the burial, the church fed the family, and I told my husband I wanted to get back to the cemetery to get pictures of the flowers before anyone else got there.

So come Monday we had to meet with the lawyer. I had to get a lawyer to protect my rights, and unfortunately, the DNA test results were presented to the judge.

"No weapon formed against me shall prosper" (Isaiah 54:17 KJV).

February 2019. As if going through this, Dad's estate, and going to court wasn't enough, I had to have skin cancer cut off my face from under my left eye. After several stitches, it healed and barely left a scar.

The end of 2019 and the first of 2020 was when COVID-19 hit everywhere. Seemed like everyone was getting sick. So many people passed away. A few I knew died, and I still can't believe they are gone. Life was so pure and sweet when I was a child. Life as I've lived it for the last few years hasn't been as sweet.

Then around March 2021 I had a spot on my breast that was suspicious that had to be biopsied and tagged. Thank you, Jesus, it was just dense tissue, not cancer. I had to be rechecked every six months after that for a while, while still going to court, trying to get everything settled on Dad's estate.

Yeah, there were a lot of *stuff* that Mom and Dad had accumulated over the years, but that is all it really was to me—*stuff*. Some things may have been worth more than others, but it all comes down to *stuff*.

The Bible warns us in Matthew 6:19–20 (NLT), where Jesus says, "Don't store up treasures here on earth, where moths eat them and rust destroys them, and where thieves break in and steal. Store your treasures in heaven, where moths and rust cannot destroy, and thieves do no break in and steal. Wherever your treasure is, there the desires of your heart will also be."

Chapter 16

THE TIME THAT FOLLOWED that dreadful day after being shell-shocked and going through the turbulent waters during this escapade, which is the only thing I can really call it at the moment, is to realize that my dad's side of the family, once they heard what had happened and what has come to light, still love me no matter what! I am still part of the family. It doesn't make a difference if I'm not blood. I still have aunts, uncles, and cousins that love me, and I love them. Even Alice's family took me in as one of their own from the very beginning of her and Dad's marriage. She even introduces me as one of her daughters, which really makes me feel special. It is so unbelievable that I have gained so many brothers and sisters and nieces and nephews. They include me and my family in their special occasions.

As I sit in my living room, curled up under a winter blanket, I can't help but review "the before and the after DNA" and "the before losing my dad" and the "after losing my dad" effects to my life.

How could such an amazing, perfect childhood with all the same players turn and tear apart so quickly and so distant from each other? How did it go from that wonderful, bright life to a dark cellar filled with nothing but pain? How could a loving family lose that most important gift—the love of family?

> *Dear Lord, I just want everyone who reads this to know they are important and they matter. The thing I'm trying to do is to show everyone that if it wasn't for God in my life, I never would have gotten through everything that I had to go through. This journey that I had to walk, I know I wasn't alone in that walk. I pray that you watch over every family member and my friends. I hope that this will touch someone or help someone that is going through anything similar so that it gives them the strength they need to keep you close because you are always there. Amen.*
>
> *Because of DNA, my God brought me through some tough stuff. No way I could have done this alone.*

Because of DNA, my Lord and Savior saved me so I could walk this road that He has laid before me.

Because of DNA, my Lord didn't throw me aside while I was a baby.

Because of DNA, I will always *praise* Your *name.*

Because of DNA, I am a child *of God!*

Despite the pain I didn't cause, the changes I didn't want, and the reality I didn't know was coming, my life can still be beautiful.

"Wait on the Lord; be of good courage, and he shall strengthen thine heart; wait, I say, on the Lord" (Psalm 27:14 KJV).

Two songs that really got me through this time in my life: "God Is in This Story" and "Your Cries Have Awoken the Master."

If you have never heard the lyrics to these songs, I encourage you to listen to them no matter what struggle you may be going through.

Personally, I found putting my story on paper not just freed me but helped me see clearly and adjust my life accordingly. I also see it as a comfort to others who have also been rejected or abandoned by some of their family. I intentionally left out a lot in this, my story, because I am now okay with not having to prove my side.

In closing…

My love is built on the Rock, steadfast, true and strong, prayerfully mimicking the love of my Savior. I also have forgiven all. It's to my advantage to forgive and a strong witness to others watching. When I die, I will leave this place without taking a handful of grudges or anger with me because I need my hands free to hold the hands of my Savior.

Through all the painful memories, one which covers them is the memory of me making a trip to Rogersville for my dad to meet an attorney to find out what we needed to do in order for my dad to do an adult adoption. After further discussion with the attorney, it was decided that my dad (biological or not) was already my dad because his name was on my birth certificate. Once I left the attorney's office and called my dad to let him know the news, we both cried happy tears.

Going through the process of Dad's estate, he had added another paragraph at the end of his will to make mention and named me as his daughter with my other two siblings, and also stated, "I consider each of these individuals to be my children, and I have named them as such… This he wrote without regard or consideration of any biological relationship or lack thereof with any of his named children."

The End

Tina Louise Jones lives in Greeneville, Tennessee, with her husband, Mike. They have two sons, Cody and Laureen Ottinger and Lily, Kevin Jones and Kacie. In her spare time, Tina loves to read, crochet, and travel.

She received diplomas from the Institute of Children's Literature in recognition of successful completion of the requisite of Study of Writing for Magazines, Beyond the Basics: Creating and Selling Short Stories and Articles.